KIDS JOURNAL THROUGH COVID19

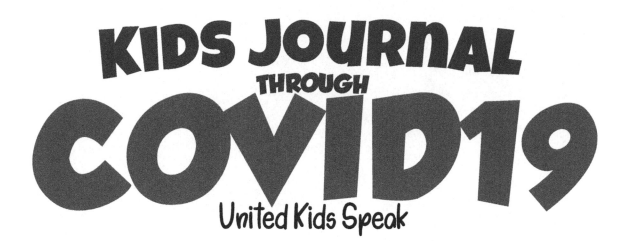

KIDS JOURNAL
THROUGH
COVID19
United Kids Speak

Laval W. Belle
& Contributing Youth Writers

Noahs Ark Publishing
Beverly Hills, California

Kids Journal Through COVID19: United Kids Speak

ISBN 978-1-7321325-7-3

Copyright (c) 2020 Laval W. Belle

Published by Noahs Ark Publishing Service

8549 Wilshire Blvd., Suite 1442
Beverly Hills, CA 90211

www.noahsarkpublishing.com

Editor: Elyse Wietstock
Cover Design: Christopher C. White
Interior Design: James Sparkman

Dedication

To parents, teachers, and educators:
You are the caretakers of our future.

Special Thanks

Ben & Jerry's

Albert and Deloise Maddox

50 States Team Leaders

Jammie Johnson

Jabari Paul

Carolyn Billups

Keecia Henderson

Patricia Canton

STATES

CHAPTERS

FOREWORD

The world was humming a different tune when I was a young girl starting off in the entertainment business in the early 1990s. While there were societal challenges that mirror some issues we experience today, our country's disposition was pretty steady and the outlook for young people was most hopeful.

Thankfully, I had the privilege of being raised by two loving and hardworking parents who indulged my creative curiosity. Their belief in me and my siblings led us to achieve wonderful artistic careers. I am grateful for this expressive outlet that continues to inspire and motivate young people across the globe.

As I read through the pages of this timely anthology these young authors have written, I am transported back to the time I was given freedom to fly artistically. Someone opened a door for me. Noahs Ark Publishing Service has opened a door for fifty young people representing fifty states in our union, to fly as they express their feelings on a topic that is challenging to the soul. With this opportunity also comes the gift of becoming a published author! Isn't that phenomenal? It is a beautifully voiced vehicle that empathizes and encourages other children who may have lost a loved one or had to be separated from them during this COVID-19 pandemic.

This current era is producing a new breed of young leaders. They are experiencing things we would have never imagined in our wildest dreams. In years to come they will talk about it firsthand. They will teach those that follow what it means to be strong, courageous and persistent. Many will urge their communities to live as wisemen, to be kindly conscious of others and protective of their environments.

Purpose boldly appeared on their doorsteps with an invitation to pursue it, and they willingly accepted. I hope this book touches the hearts of all ages in new and nostalgic ways. May it breathe life into and revive your spirit of servanthood, that you may assist your communities with talents bestowed upon you!

– **Tamera Mowry-Housley**

7 THE SEVEN-YEAR-OLDS

Gianna Pink Floyd

TEXAS

I have been playing and riding around with my auntie. When I go out I now have to always wear my mask, use hand sanitizer, and make sure I wash my hands for 20 seconds. I also make sure I practice social distancing. When we have house gatherings I don't get to see everybody because we have to be socially distant. I stay at home a lot and play games in the house with my mom and auntie. During COVID-19 my Daddy, George Floyd, changed the world.

Faith Adeniran

MARYLAND

I had fun going outside to play with my sisters, we would go to school in the school bus and go to church on Sundays. But in December coronavirus hit Wuhan, China, and gradually moved to other parts of the country till it went around the world. When the virus hit the

United States the government had to shut all borders from allowing people to come into the country, and to also reduce the rate at which the virus was spreading. The government looked for a better way to keep everyone safe by asking us to stay at home. Due to this, we could not go to school, we had to be homeschooled. We could not go to our friends to play and they could not come to ours. I did not have a good time at home because all we did was stay at home. Coronavirus has killed lots of people because there is no cure yet. When we are at home we use a Chromebook for online classes and the only place we could play was in the garage, basement, and sometimes ride our bicycle in front of the house or take a walk with grandparents. It was not fun at all, my little sister wanted to go to the playground all the time, but mom said no, that coronavirus was everywhere. There have been some things that we have been asked to do in order to prevent coronavirus. These are: We have to wash our hands for twenty or thirty seconds each time we feel we have touched something we are not supposed to, or when we come back in the house from any outing. We cannot hug, no hi-fives, we should only do fist-bumps and elbow greetings. When we sneeze, we should sneeze in our elbow and cough in a paper towel and trash it immediately. We should also stay home when we do not feel well. My mom is the only person that goes to do groceries, that way we can have food to eat in the house. My grandma and grandpa cannot travel to Nigeria because the airplanes are not flying, they have been staying in the house as well. It is boring staying at home. I miss going to school and the different fun activities that we have, like field trips and playing with my friends at recess. We also missed the end of the school year jamboree. I miss Girl Scouts weekly activities and other fun activities like camping, end of the year field trips, and being with the other Girl Scouts. I still try to have fun at home by playing games with my sisters, watching movies, and riding my bike around the neighborhood. I am hoping that coronavirus will be over soon, so that we can all go back to our normal lives.

Aubrey Lewis

NEW YORK

Coronavirus was a good experience for me. I got to stay home and spend more time with my family. I got a new teacher, and he invited me to Fun Friday to play games and watch movies. My schoolwork was kind of hard, I had too much work! Sometimes I felt sad because I had to play by myself. I played games on the computer with my friends, playing games online made me feel better. We also had a dance contest to our favorite song. Some people got sick and died from the coronavirus. That made me feel bad because that could have been my family member. God is a spirit and I pray for the people that died and their family. I hope that everyone stays safe from the coronavirus.

Solomon Robertson

NORTH CAROLINA

How COVID-19 has impacted me: Overall, it hasn't really affected me. I miss my learning time with my school friends and my teachers. I feel sad that I have to stay home every day, and for me that's boring. I've been learning coding on Scratch, and sometimes I still get to play with my neighbor friends. That's not the same as playing with my friends at school though. I haven't really been impacted, but I am sad that we can't actually talk and be together with people.

I'm a little upset that we have to do everything by computer, and we can't hug each other. I miss the friends that I love and know. I miss family too. Now it's just all on video. I miss everyone I know.

When I get to see everyone, I want to celebrate! We can eat pizza and cupcakes, with some apple juice. We can have a dance party, color, and we can hug each other. You can't do that online because if you stand up or move, they can't even see you on the screen! I like talking to people in person. I don't want to always look at a screen or a device. It's hard to show our ideas when we are not in person.

I'm just not comfortable in quarantine. I don't really feel safe. Like when I play with my neighbors, I know I'm not supposed to. We don't social distance when we play, and I don't want to die. I don't want to get really sick; I just want to play.

We've been doing really well though, in our house. We don't really go out, and when we do, we wear our masks. Plus, we have back up masks in the car in case we forget. So, I'm pretty sure we aren't going to die. Well, everybody dies at some time, but just not now, from COVID. We have to be really healthy in case we do get sick! Everybody should grow a garden and eat lots of vegetables and do heart-happy moving. You know what I think? I think that people that get sick and are still alive are healthy. And the people that die are already sick. So, when the coronavirus comes in like BOOM! They are just too sick and die.

We gotta stay safe and healthy, because health is wealth. I learned that from a video on Scratch. You need money to stay healthy, so you can buy seeds and stuff to grow a farm. But no cows, we should make our own milk, and drink lots of water. You need to buy some elderberry and vitamins, and always, always wash your hands!

THE
EIGHT-YEAR-OLDS

Jonnette S. Yancy
and Tosha J. Freeman

RHODE ISLAND

COVID-19 is a very bad virus, and there are people that are dying. There are many reasons why COVID-19 is bad and makes us sad. It's hard for people to stay away from sick people. It's hard for people to go to places, because they have to stay six feet apart and some stores have a lot of people. Any family members that are sick have to be taken care of at the hospital, and some people die at the hospital.

Staying six feet apart from our classmates is going to be hard because we have to work together. We can't sit too close to each other when it's time for math, reading, or other schoolwork. Some kids die from COVID-19. Some of our family members passed away because of COVID-19. We can't see people that we love and care about because they might have COVID-19. You have to ask if they're sick, so you can stay six feet away. We have to wash our hands for at least one to two minutes, even for lunch and dinner, to make sure that there are no germs. COVID-19 is serious and it has affected us all in some way.

People have to work together, stay clean, stay safe, and wear a mask. We'll get through this.

Mehki Peterson

VIRGINIA

I was scared when I had to get a test for COVID-19 because I have asthma. I had a bad asthma attack, and had to go to the hospital. They gave me medicine to feel better. The next day I had to go to the doctor, and they stuck a long Q-tip down my throat and up my nose. It hurt very bad. But I was glad that I did not have COVID-19 after my results came back. The coronavirus is so bad and I wish it would go away.

Mia Connolly

NEW HAMPSHIRE

My experience with COVID-19 has been both boring and fun. It has been boring because I don't have any friends to play with. I have an older brother, and he is seventeen, but he will not play with me. It has been fun because I can play on my phone, and not worry too much about school. Sometimes, I have planned when to FaceTime my friends or stay up late. I wish COVID-19 was not as big of a deal, like we could still wear masks and I could go back to hanging out with my friends, so I could hug them!

THE NINE-YEAR-OLDS

Yackiel E. Candelaria Rosa

PUERTO RICO

The illness of coronavirus has changed us so much. My parents tell me that because of the virus, I have to go to school online. I miss my friends a little. What I miss about school is doing experiments in class, they were fun and we would laugh a lot. I really miss my teacher Mrs. Santiago because she would read stories and play fun videos on the computer. She is the best teacher in the world. Before the coronavirus I would play basketball all the time. Because of the coronavirus I can't play in the Tournament of Colors. What I really like the most is to sing and act, because I want to be an actor when I grow up. When the coronavirus is over I want to film a movie. Since I'm home, I didn't get sick. The coronavirus scares me because it can live in the lungs and won't allow us to breathe and we can die. I am upset because my brother puts his hands in his mouth and he could get sick. Then he could touch me and I could get sick, and I especially don't want him to get me sick. I want COVID to go away so we can go out without a mask. I don't like wearing the mask because it's hard for me to breathe, it hurts my ears, and it's uncomfortable to wear them. When the coronavirus goes away, I will be free to go to Wal-Mart and buy toys and cassettes. I am going to buy a Beyblade, Nerf guns and cassettes for my Switch. These are action and adrenaline games and I love them. I will be glad when this virus goes away. But until it's gone, I am grateful for my life and health.

Alyviah Joi Reed

ALASKA

When I first noticed COVID-19, I was already tired of staying in the house from being on spring break. Spring break was getting ready to end, and my mom came home from work talking to us about COVID-19. Our spring break ended up getting extended for another two weeks, so basically all of March we were in the house. Then my mom told me that we can learn at home and do schoolwork on our own. Mom made a daily schedule for my brother King and I. We had to get up at 7:00 a.m. like a normal school day. We had family bible study, exercise time, schoolwork time, play time, chores, and relax and nap time too. It seemed like a good idea, but I got really bored quickly. A little bit of time passed and we were told to "hunker down," which meant we really couldn't go anywhere. The streets were quiet. When we did leave the house, Mom made us all strip down, put our clothes in the washer and we had to immediately wash hands, face, and shower. We wiped down our groceries with Lysol wipes. We made our own hand sanitizer too. Because my brother and I have been diagnosed with asthma and allergies, Mom made sure we took it very seriously that everything we touched was sanitized and clean!

So, April rolls around and we end up doing our Zoom meetings with our class and teachers all the way to June. Stores started to open back up, but the twist is, you have to wear a mask. This made things better because I was able to go outside and not be stuck in the house. I really dislike COVID-19, because people are getting sick and dying! I celebrated my birthday during this tragic time. Even though I couldn't go anywhere--not the park, not to school, or to play outside with my friends--no real birthday party, I am still grateful to be alive. I'm very sad for my sister who graduated from high school this year. My mom had planned so much for her and us for the summer. I can't go see my dad and siblings because he is in another state, and I can't travel to see them. Staying in the house is boring, but I enjoy doing puzzles, potting plants with Mom, reading books, drawing and coloring, and making up activities to do with my family. I just wish COVID-19 would end with God taking it away.

I am ready to go back to school and see my friends. I want to travel and be able to go to church, to go places without wearing a mask or being worried about distancing myself. I just want life to go back to normal. I'm not sure what normal is, but I'm sure God does, and He will figure it out.

Coronavirus can make you sick, and some people might even die. We stay in our houses, stay six feet away from people, and wear masks too. I have to FaceTime friends and family, we can't go to school so we go on Zoom, and only twenty-five people can go into the store at one time. It's okay, I guess. I'm okay with not having to go to school because I don't get bullied anymore, and I like the programs I'm in on Zoom. They're fantastic, we get to watch cool videos, play math games, and do fun activities online. I FaceTime my friends and cousins to play games. The part I don't like is that we don't get to see our friends in person, and you have to stay away from people you love.

On my birthday, my mom and my big sister Aaliyah threw me a surprise party on Zoom. It was the best, all of my family was there! I got a trampoline, a keyboard, skates, Legos, and my mom made me a lemon cake. For Eid, we prayed in the house and saw other people pray on the Zoom in the parking lot. We even had a car parade that went from my house to the Masjid. Everybody decorated their cars, and we got out and took pictures with our friends and other Muslims with masks on. I got more toys and we watched movies and ate a lot of good food. My mom lets me jump on the trampoline and skate in the house, I like that.

Kimathi A. Robinson

SOUTH CAROLINA

Since the quarantine began, I have missed being with a lot of people. I miss my classmates and my school because we had a lot of fun. I miss spending time with my family and friends. Some of my family live far away and we are not able to visit each other. I have not seen my Uncle Titus or my Aunt Courtney in a long time. I do call Aunt Courtney. Sometimes she calls me, or we text each other to keep in touch. My grandmother lives an hour away and because of COVID I have not seen her as often, because she is elderly and could catch COVID easily from me.

Since the COVID-19 quarantine started, there have not been many drumming and performing events. I really love drumming and miss doing this a lot. I cannot go to the Plex, the library, nor to my friends' homes. When I go to my friends' homes now, we have to stay outside to play. When it was my birthday, I could not have my friends over. Instead, my mom and I walked to their homes and offered them cupcakes to celebrate with me.

COVID-19 has changed my life in a lot of little ways. For instance, I cannot play with my friends from church without a mask due to social distancing, and we cannot touch each other. I visited my school a few weeks ago and realized how much I missed everyone there. Because of COVID-19 I could no longer go to a physical school building and had to go to classes online, which was really hard for me. At times I am happy that COVID-19 happened, because I do not worry about having my games interrupted. Sometimes, I am bored because my sisters are much older than I am and do not play with me, and often my friends cannot come out to play. Before COVID-19 I used to play baseball on a team, but when COVID-19 hit we had to stop playing because our park closed down. I was sad because I was so ready to have a fun and winning season on the team.

COVID-19 has made my family spend more time together. During this time we painted pictures as a family. While painting my picture I learned that painting was a good way to calm myself. My sisters, my mom, and I had a kickball game one day. I was teamed with my sister and we played hard. We did not win but it was still fun. It is good spending time with my family. We have learned a lot about each other in this time. I even tried to learn how to crochet. That did not work out too well, but my mom started making my blanket for me.

COVID-19 has shown me that although things are shut down, I can have fun in my own neighborhood. I have met other kids in my complex who I would not usually play with. I made a really good friend, Kamden who I talk to every day. COVID-19 has brought about a lot of changes; some good, some bad.

Della Connor

VERMONT

Before COVID-19, every day at school my friends and I played games like Capture the Flag and kickball. I attend a small school with only thirty to forty students in it, and when we went outside everybody played together. It was a lot of fun. I love to be involved in sports, and my day would include basketball, and in some seasons swim teams. All of that has changed.

Now we stay at home, and when we are out with other people, we wear masks, stay six feet apart, and have to be careful so people like my mother don't catch the virus. Staying at home is not a problem for me, I love my home. I practice basketball every day, and play with my parents. My dad is really tall, and my mom is a great player, but I think I might have the edge because I am fast.

Before COVID, I would go to my friend's homes and we would talk, play, giggle, and spend time together. Now I chat with them on my tablet, but I know it is not going to be this way forever. I have mixed emotions about this pandemic. I know some people don't have safe and good homes to be in, and that makes me sad. I do miss the active life I had before, but I love being with my family too.

If this were all to go away tomorrow, we would make plans. My mom and I want to go to the beach with my grandparents. We want to get our nails done, and go to New York City to see the shows and wonderful places to visit.

Thank you for wanting to hear from kids. We are going through this too. We have to figure out ways to be safe and still have fun. I could even share some ideas with kids like me who don't have brothers or sisters to play with. If I could speak to all nine-year-old kids right now I would say, "Take it one day at a time, and make the best of each day."

Bentlee Thivierge

IDAHO

My COVID-19 experience has been bad. I don't like homeschooling, and I can't wait to go back to school. I miss my friends, and I miss going on trips with my family. We have gotten to go camping, which was fun. My school shut down in March and we did packets for homeschool. My mom got to stay home with me for a month. I would've liked to be in school. I love school. I really liked my teacher and missed him. I really hope we get to stay in school.

Max Cobb Bell

OHIO

This is how my quarantine is going. Online school was pretty good. I was able to talk to my friends and still get in my education. The hardest part about online school was we used eight different applications and sometimes my work would not submit. It was hard to keep up with the requirements. My teacher was helpful because she gave us office hours to ask questions. Our librarian Mrs. Kaylor (my godmom) read books to us on YouTube, and encouraged us to read every day. Our school counselor had office hours too, and I told my friends about it.

I first heard about the coronavirus before Christmas break, from YouTube. I kept telling people about the coronavirus, but no one was listening. I even got sanitizer from Bath and Body Works that I could carry in my backpack to keep my hands clean. The scent was called Noir and it had a cool turtle case. When we first heard that we were going to have to leave the school and work from home, I was happy! But when I learned that the virus was making people sick and killing people, it made me sad. We got a huge packet of work from school that took forever to complete. I was supposed to be on spring break, but my family insisted that I do my work first. It was hard to stay in the house with the shutdown, so we went walking on the trails near the house to get fresh air and exercise. I remember it even snowed on the first Sunday, when we could not go to church.

My aunt Michelle made me about four masks to wear whenever I leave the house. Let's just say they are hard to keep up with. My strategy for wearing my mask to school is to keep it with my eyeglasses and hopefully hold on to both all day. Social distancing will be hard because I am a people person. I like to talk a lot and tell stories. I also like to play basketball and rap and spend time with people. I have been able to spend time with some of my family, but only a small group at a time. I hope that there is a vaccine and cure for the virus soon. We will always remember this time, but I hope it does not happen again. I am praying for the number of new cases to go down so we can go back to school and not have to wear masks. I have been practicing my dribbling and shooting, and was looking forward to trying out for the fourth-grade basketball team. So many dreams on hold until we figure out how to manage the virus.

Roosevelt Lewis III

TENNESSEE

When COVID-19 caused school to shut down, I was really sad because I was not able to see my friends. But then, COVID-19 became more. It meant no birthday parties, no more friends coming over, and more being bored and quarantined.

COVID-19 is very intense for people who have lost family and friends to the disease. COVID-19 is very bad but if we all band together, then I believe we can, no we will, defeat COVID-19 once and for all!

THE TEN-YEAR-OLDS

DaJoan Lee Harrington

TEXAS

Friday, March 13th, 2020 changed my entire fourth grade school year. This day was special because spring break started at the end of the day school bell. But on this Friday, my mom said, "DJ, you don't have school today." Somewhat confused, I began getting ready to start my day, with tons of questions going through my mind. Mom told me we would talk about it in the car. On our way to my aunt's, my mom said, "Remember last night on the news when they were speaking about the coronavirus?" I replied, "Yes." Mom said, "Well the schools are concerned with your safety and have decided that you will not return until after spring break." At ten years old, my most concerning question was, "What am I going to do for spring break?" At that point, my mom had no answers other than "We will have to see."

March 16th, 2020, the first day of spring break, it was announced: No Boys and Girls Club. I was devastated. I won't get to see my friends? We had basketball games and dance battles planned. How was this going to work? All Mom could do was attempt to ease my mind and tell me everything would work out, later to tell me she really had no answers. She told me that she knew that the coronavirus could affect me severely, due to my asthma, so she kept me close. Mom took every precaution necessary; purchasing sanitizer, more cleaning supplies, and masks. During the week, I had the chance to visit my grandparents, but little did I know there wouldn't be any more hugs, kisses, and high fives. I am a hugger, and my grands play a huge role in my life, so this affected me dearly. I like to be under the people I love, their affection makes me feel secure. The first Thursday of spring break, I went to my karate class. During class, Grand Master Williams stated, "Today is your last class until further notice." My heart sank. Why is all of this happening? Why is it everything I love, I feel like I am losing? That evening, my mom was listening to the news, as she does often, and we both heard, AISD will be closed indefinitely. "Mom, what is indefinitely?" I asked. She said, "Until further notice?" Again, another bombshell. No spring break, no camp, no church, no karate, and now no school. What does all of this mean? Where am I supposed to go? How will I end fourth grade?

Mom, again in an attempt to ease my mind, said, "It will all work out." She told me, she would be able to work from home and she was going to be my teacher. I laughed hysterically, because I remember thinking of just doing homework with her and how frustrated she would get when I would tell her the answer was wrong. She told me that she would use her resources and ensure we understood what was supposed to happen. It took a few weeks to get up and running, but we came up with a schedule that worked. I told her by week three, I wanted to be homeschooled, then *she* laughed hysterically, saying, "That is not going to happen." I found it hard to cope with not seeing my friends, teachers, and some of the administration, but I understand the reason behind it.

We stopped going to the church and everything was online. That was pretty cool, because by 12 p.m. on Sunday our day was complete, and we could just hang out. Normal Sunday dinners changed; we could only do drive-bys to my grandparents' house. We would have to make plates and return home, not spending more than twenty minutes with them. There was no Easter Sunday, no Mother's Day, no birthday celebrations. My emotions were all over the place. I was confused, angry, hurt, tired, and I just wanted to know when everything was going to go back to the way it was. Mom said, "Baby, this is our new normal. We will adjust and get through it."

In a matter of two and half months, my life changed in a big way. I went from being a social butterfly to practically not being social at all; wearing a mask everyone I go; FaceTiming everyone so I can see them and they can see me; having classes on Zoom; watching church on Facebook; and having to compete in karate tournaments online rather than in person. This has been a transition, but I am grateful that I have my family to get through it with. I continue to hear and see #AloneTogether and I hope that everyone has somebody they can get through this with.

T'Vonn Natel Parchman Jr.

PENNSYLVANIA

I love to play football, basketball, and any sports where I can run, jump, and push people without getting in trouble. My mom says I have a lot of energy and playing sports is a way for me to get rid of some of it. I am good at all the sports I play. I love when my family comes and watches me, I try to play hard so that they will clap and be proud of me. I have not been able to play outside as much as I could before the coronavirus came to Pennsylvania. Now I can only be around my family, and I can't see any of my friends. Since coronavirus, life has not been very good. It's hard to enjoy my summer, since I am not able to do everything I like to do in the summertime. My parents say that life is not good for a lot of people. A lot of people have been getting sick, and some have died. That's not good and it makes me sad. I was very sad when I heard that. We can't go to school right now, but I hope I will be able to go back to school someday. It's been hard staying at home for a long time without going anywhere, but at least we are all hanging in there. At least we are all having fun with each other. I have enjoyed spending time with my brothers and sister. We try to have birthday parties even if it's just my family. As we try to get through this time, we need a lot of heart. I also heard that a man was killed but it was not coronavirus, it was because he was black. I hope that people learn that someone should not die because they are black. I am black and my dad is black, and we are nice.

Sofia J. Jenkins

MINNESOTA

This is how COVID-19 has affected my life in good and bad ways. When school was cancelled and we started online school, it took me some time to get used to it and figure it all out. Good thing my parents were able to help out and learn about fourth grade again, my dad told me it had been a long time since he was in fourth grade. When the online school finished, I felt a little sad because I wouldn't see my friends. The class meetings online were fun, and I was going to miss them. Before COVID-19 I didn't love art, I mean I liked it, but it wasn't my favorite. Maybe because I wasn't very good at it, but with all of the social distancing and everything closed, I kept trying and trying. After a while, I started to love it and got a lot better at it also! It is one of my favorite things to do now. Since I had a lot of time with everyone at home because of COVID-19, I tried my "green thumb," as my dad calls it. We planted a tomato plant named Herbert. I only have one at the moment, but we will plant more. He has already started to grow tomatoes and gotten really big! With all of this time, I had the chance to try some new things and found out that I'm good at some things I never would have tried. Also some things that I'm not good at, but that's okay it was still fun to try. I feel sad for all of the people sick with COVID-19 and wish it would all be over soon!

Tahji Edmond

NEVADA

My mom told me about the virus when we could not go to school one day. I learned it was very dangerous, it got really bad and they had to close the school down and stay home. I could not go outside as much as we like to. We have to wear masks, wash our hands a lot, and stay quarantined to stay safe. I cannot do the same activities I used to, like getting on the bus for school. I feel bored because I cannot play with my friends. There is hardly anyone outside anymore. I have one friend that my mom allows me to play with at my house. We all have to stay inside, and I do things on my phone and tablet mostly.

My friend comes over and we play video games, but before the virus we would go to the playground, stay outside and play tag, or go places near my house. We used to go swimming every day, but now I can't go as much as I used to. I usually go swimming every day because it is hot in the summer. I miss all my friends.

We cannot go to school because it is closed. I attend distant learning. We work with the teacher on the computer through Google Classroom. I get to see my classmates, and we talk on video chat. We cover math, science, social studies, and other things. We have homework, but it's different. The teacher asks us questions and we answer on video chat. She corrects us and send the information to our parents. I like distance-learning, but I would rather go to school like normal because we are not all together on the computer. I attend a magnet school and our class is kind of small, maybe twenty-something classmates. I miss my robotics team and wish we could go back to school.

I feel sad and bummed out because we can barely do anything. We can't go to school, the virus is spreading, I cannot physically see my friends, we have to stay six feet apart. I would like to go to school, but I'm afraid because the virus is really small and we cannot see if it's there. It will probably be December, when it will be very cold, before we know about school.

King Peoples

CALIFORNIA

COVID-19 is horrible if you get infected. People make jokes, but there is nothing funny about it if you get it. The way to stay safe from COVID-19 is to wash your hands, wear a mask in public, and stay six feet from people you don't know.

COVID-19 has affected my family in the way that we have to live, by not being able to go on vacations, or visit my grandmother in the nursing home. No one in my family has gotten it, but we make sure that we wash our hands, not be in crowds, and wear face masks when we go out. My fear about COVID-19 is someone in my family getting it. My mom just had my baby sister in November 2019, and I'm scared she might get it at a very young age.

I miss school a little bit, but I miss my friends the most. I miss being able to play and go to the Boys and Girls Club. From being at home,

I have learned that it is good to be around your family more and appreciate them. I have a good family and I am glad because some kids have to stay at home and they don't have a good family. While I have been in quarantine, I have found new TV shows to watch. I don't like that everything is virtual. I am enrolled in a virtual STEAM camp and I am waiting to see if it will be as fun as going to a regular camp.

I think COVID-19 is going to end if the scientists get a vaccine or a cure. I think it is going to end in 2021, around June.

Abigail Spenny

WYOMING

Ugg, COVID-19 stank. How does it make you feel? For me, it stinks. I had to do dance on Zoom.

Well, I am kind of happy because I had nothing to do for the talent show, but I was also sad because we were supposed to open a restaurant, and well... quarantine shut that down. My mom said she saw people fighting over toilet paper. We also have to wear masks everywhere and use hand sanitizer constantly.

When the coronavirus happened, schools closed. Some parents had no idea what to do with their kids. I had to stay at home with my little brother, and no friends.

I am so glad that Boys & Girls Club opened up, at least we haven't seen people fighting over toilet paper. We still have to constantly use hand sanitizer, but now there is more family time for me and at least I got to be independent.

Kevin Bennett

FLORIDA

My experience with the coronavirus has been challenging. First, it is scary. COVID-19 can target anyone. Next, I could not go anywhere, everyone must stay home. Lastly, I could not go to school. I have never felt like this, I am afraid that I will get sick and die.

Worrying about my family is scary, too. My parents, brother, and grandparents can get this virus and become very sick. This virus travels person to person. I can't believe this is happening.

Being home is fun, but not all the time. We cannot go places. We can't go to the movies, visit family and friends, or go to church. I miss playing basketball and football with my team. We can talk on the phone, Skype, and FaceTime. If we do come together, we must stay six feet apart. That's called social distancing.

Lastly, all students had to stay home. This was to prevent us from catching the virus. We all became homeschoolers. Staying home was fun, but I missed my classmates. I missed playing and having fun. My class got a new teacher, Mrs. Cousins. We met virtually. It was kind of cool, but I wish I could have met her in person.

I liked getting up late in the morning and having my morning meetings with Mrs. Cousins. After, I would do my assignments, play, and do some assignments again. I enjoyed being a homeschooler, but I don't think my mother would agree. We are the first class to graduate from elementary to middle school virtually! That's pretty cool! I can't wait to see how life is going to be after this pandemic.

Trinity Pace

GEORGIA

COVID-19 has changed a lot of things that I am used to doing. I have missed seeing my friends every day. Although I can see them on Zoom and FaceTime, we can't go to the pool because of COVID-19.

When I do Zoom calls with my class, it is very fun. Sometimes we do scavenger hunts by grabbing things in our house. Online class was fun, you can pace yourself with work. For exploratory, we were able to pick different activities for each class.

Most of the assignments were easy. Some reading passages were very interesting, and some science assignments were cool to do. My class had a "All About ME" project to do. We did it for our student teacher.

My brother and I play a bunch of games together. We've made videos for church and teacher appreciation week. I ride my new bike a few days a week. Most days I just want to relax and watch TV. My brother just won't leave me alone, so I must spend a lot of time playing with him. Sometimes I miss just going in stores and window shopping.

Also, I get to spend more time with my mom and dad. My dad explained to me what he does at work. I have been thinking a lot about what's going on in the world. All this police brutality and racism is making me think about my future. Nobody should have to go through that.

I get to talk to my friends on Snapchat, FaceTime, Zoom, and text. My friend and I played truth or dare over the phone a few weeks ago. Sometimes my family goes to Amerson Park. We ride our bikes or walk around. I have been binge-watching many shows on Netflix and Tubi.

My brother and I have played a lot of Roblox. We also recreated some games in real life. My birthday is coming up, so I must think of alternative plans. I might have a sleepover with very close friends. These past few weeks I have been staying up very late. I got a bead kit and a string kit. With this, I can make bead bracelets whenever I want.

I hope that the COVID-19 virus goes away. I wish we could see our friends. I pray that all the police brutality goes away. Just to wrap it up, I hope everything goes away and everybody is safe.

Reggie Butler

OKLAHOMA

I first found out about the coronavirus in the middle of the school year. I like to call it "Corona." I heard people saying it was deadly, and I was worried about getting sick. I had heard that it makes your throat, stomach, or head hurt. One time, I almost thought I had "the Corona." I was scared because my throat and head were hurting. My parents told me I didn't have it because I didn't have a fever, and it went away that day. I was happy that school was cancelled and we had no homework. I was happy to just stay home. I played with my brother and sister a lot. We played Monopoly, and I remember laughing when we ran inside and my sister slipped because of her socks. Then the quarantine got boring because everything was closed, and we couldn't go anywhere. I saw my friends using Zoom and we did some scavenger hunts. It was bad when there was no End of School parties or Super Kid's Day. Wearing masks all the time is frustrating, because I feel like I can't breathe with it on my nose. I would get mad when our trips had to be cancelled. The saddest part about "Corona" was when some of my family got coronavirus. My great-aunt died from coronavirus. I was sad. I remember when she gave me a puppy and I liked riding the horse at her house. If I could change coronavirus, I would make it smaller than colds and every sickness. I would make it to where it's not deadly and people don't get sick.

11

THE ELEVEN-YEAR-OLDS

Lauryn Coleman

MISSOURI

The year 2020 began with a bang. The city of Kansas City has been waiting for nearly fifty years to celebrate a KC Chiefs' Super Bowl win. Approximately 100,000 people gathered on a cold snowy day and flooded the parade route to catch a quick glimpse of their favorite Chiefs player. After the celebrations ended, the devastation began. In March, across the country, the news continued to provide alarming numbers about the coronavirus, or COVID-19. This incurable virus has claimed the lives of people near and far. My life as a fifth grader would change forever.

As of March 29th, 2020, I would not return to my classroom as I did before COVID-19. I would be forced to continue my learning via virtual classes. My experience with virtual learning has been frustrating, boring, and difficult. I feel this way because it is difficult to manage a regular class schedule and have corrections, plus making sure that you are on time to your classes. Technology is key to being able to come to school every day. So if your Wi-Fi isn't working, then you are going to miss some of the class and potentially important information. But if we had in-person school we wouldn't have those problems. If I were headmaster of the school or even the principal, I would consider less homework. This would avoid late work and provide teachers an easier experience when grading assignments.

My summers are usually spent running, swimming, and being with friends and family. Although this summer has been different, I have learned some very important things: to be extra careful about germs, and to wash your hands properly. Also, ensuring you wear a mask when entering a store or gas station. Masks, hand sanitizing, and social distancing are the new normal.

COVID-19 has affected my family, my learning, and my extracurricular activities. However, I refuse to allow COVID-19 to deter me from my goals. In fact, it has increased my desire to continue working hard to become a pediatric emergency room doctor. To all the doctors working on the front line, you have illustrated a beautiful picture of hard work and sacrifice.

As the Kansas City Chiefs prepare for the upcoming 2020 football season, I am reminded of the memories from the celebration parade. Winners, such as doctors and other front-line workers, share the same heart and soul as those champions. I am excited to see how the home team will raise the bar, exceed expectations, and win back-to-back Super Bowl titles.

Jaylynn Hawes

DELAWARE

Imagine having an amazing school year, honor roll grades, great teachers, awesome friends, and then Friday, March 13th, 2020 happened. That was my last day of the school year because of COVID-19. My amazing school year changed to a horrifying virtual nightmare. I felt like I learned so much more when I was in school. Most of my assignments I had to complete on my own, without much teacher interaction. My teachers, Mr. Mac and Mrs. Treadwell, were great at actually explaining a lot of the new skills they were teaching. Having online school is definitely not for me! Being locked in the house for almost four months is really exhausting.

Getting used to quarantine has been a challenge, and I'm learning to adjust so far. I really miss my family, but I communicate with them through our "Family Zoom Time" when we meet every other Sunday to catch up on the latest family news. Four of my family members had the coronavirus. My nana, two of my aunts, and my gramps caught the virus. My nana and aunt work at a local hospital, and the virus kind of spread throughout their house. The ironic thing is just a week before they tested positive, my aunt came to our house for a visit, but my mom wouldn't let her in. Oh boy! We were all glad my mom didn't open the door! My uncle was the only one in their household that did not get the coronavirus. It's heartbreaking that my gramps spent weeks in the hospital, and passed away on July 2nd.

Another challenge to being in quarantine is not being able to dance in four months. I miss my dance teachers and team members. I miss flagging, and the three-to-four-hour rehearsals (well not really); but I do miss our dance performances. So to replace the time I've missed from church, I am currently participating in a virtual summer camp. I get to make recipes, keep up on skills in a fun way, and chat with friends. Last summer, the camp met in person, and I worked hard along with other campers to earn a trip to California to meet some really famous people like Debbie Allen and her dance studio! The trip was planned for April of this year during Easter break, but coronavirus ruined it all!

During these hard days, I entertain myself by painting, which is one of my hobbies. I like to draw and create sketches. I play with my four-year-old sister sometimes! I love the people I live with, but I'm sorry to break it to you, I need my own space every now and then. Nevertheless, I'm grateful to be with my family every day. I am grateful that my parents are keeping us safe. I'll be grateful when the coronavirus is gone!

Donald Parham

INDIANA

This is my quick essay about COVID-19. So here we go. This COVID experience has been hard on me, and not just me. The pandemic has affected a lot of people, and animals too. Pets are having to go through their owners having COVID. This is hard on everyone, and I have a lot of mixed feelings. This is the worst thing ever and we should all deal with this, but this book is about a personal opinion (I think). I think that COVID is ruining lives, and there are people who have it a lot worse than me. I hope that this will end soon.

This has given me and probably a lot of others cabin fever. This is a bad way to spend our time. But there is good news. People have the time to clean up more, but let's save that till the end. For me I've been cooped up in my house too long. I feel horrible about this. And for anyone who feels the same way, it's fine, there are a lot of ways to cope. But my overall opinion is: COVID SUCKS. But not completely. COVID has ruined lives, and even ended them, but it actually helps us be more human. We have free time that we normally wouldn't have. Now what are we going to do with this free time? Focus on COVID, or go be a human?

There are a lot of cons to this, and they all block out all of the pros except one: Free time. The pro isn't great, but it's all we got for now. The cons try to ruin it, but can't. COVID may end and ruin lives, but we have to get our minds off of COVID. Do the daily routines, but play a game, take a walk, do something. COVID may be ruining lives, but we can better our lives. There are a lot of things we can't do, but still we can do this.

Robert Powell

SOUTH DAKOTA

The COVID-19 pandemic has been a hard experience for everyone in this world. Here is my experience.

I remember when I first started hearing about it on the news, how people were spreading the virus through travel. I was not scared until they started mentioning how people were dying from the infection. I remember thinking, "What is a pandemic?" I read and watched videos through school about pandemics and other viruses from the past. At my school, my teachers explained that we did not have any cases here, but we needed to be careful. We were told to cough or sneeze into our elbow, to limit contact with each other, and to wash our hands as much as possible. We also helped to wipe down counters, desks, and handles with disinfectant wipes. The last day I was in school, my teacher told us we might not be coming back the next week. At first this was kind of exciting, but it quickly became scary and upsetting.

The virus started spreading in the US, and my sister and brother and I were no longer allowed to go into stores, play with friends, or see our grandparents. Our spring season soccer and swimming lessons were cancelled. We started online learning after one week, and it was more challenging than being in school. Our school is a Spanish immersion school, so it was hard to be without teachers to motivate and help us with our work as they usually do. I was worried about my grandparents when the news started talking about the risk in people sixty-five years old and up. I also worried about my mom and dad going to work because their patients could have the virus and spread it.

Over the summer, because we did not have too many cases in South Dakota, we were allowed to see some friends and to go into stores with masks. We can also see our grandparents outside while wearing masks. Our school is reopening at the end of August and I am excited to see my friends and teachers. I have read about the precautions our school is taking, but I am still worried someone will get sick or that school will be cancelled. My grandma asked me the same thing she had asked my cousins: "Would you rather go to school for one full month in person or for one week online?" I said, "One full month in person." My cousins have all said the same thing.

Dacia Givens

NEW MEXICO

The way COVID-19 has affected me is I really love school. I miss running, seeing my friends, and hanging out with them during recess. Being quarantined in my house has been lonely and sad. I miss having person-to-person contact. My teacher also asked me to choose the song and make up the end of the year dance for our end of year performance. Due to COVID-19, it all got cancelled. It makes me feel sad, I really would have enjoyed that opportunity. I also was in a dance class, which I enjoyed very much. I would go every week on Wednesday. I made amazing friends there, who I miss so much. We talk on the phone, but it's not the same as when we got to laugh and joke in person. My Nana, my mom, and I have a family tradition where every other week we would go watch a movie at the movie theater. Recently my mom told me the theater has been closed for good. It feels like we lost something so special. The movie theater will have such amazing memories. COVID-19 has been an emotional rollercoaster. Some days I am happy, and some days I am so sad. Some days I feel scared, and some days I don't know what to think.

When we leave our house, we grab our masks and hand sanitizer. That's all new to me. I don't understand much about the seriousness of this virus, but I know it's changed my life. We go to the grocery store and before we climb out of the car we put on gloves and a mask, and my mom carries a hand sanitizer in her purse. She makes me use it before we go into the store. While I am in the store, she keeps me in the basket with my sunglasses on. It makes me feel sad, I miss feeling free and not scared all the time. When we leave the store, we climb back in the car and my mom passes around the hand sanitizer again. I get upset, but my mom says it's for our safety because she is trying to keep me healthy and safe. When we get to my house, my mom makes me change my shoes and clothes so that she can wash them. COVID-19 has truly changed everything. I can't go visit my family. My mom says it's so we don't make my aunties, uncles, ninos, ninas, and cousins sick. I really miss my cousins. I sit in my room and write to them, waiting for the day we can be together again. In my art class I painted a picture, and my art teacher chose it to be in an art exhibit. She was going to try to get it in an art exhibit at this year's New Mexico State Fair, but COVID-19 has cancelled that too. I feel like my hard work this year has been taken away from me. For mine and my mom's birthday, which is in April, we were planning a trip to Circus Circus in Las Vegas Nevada, but the virus cancelled our trip. This virus has made me sad, hurt, mad, heartbroken, and lonely. I miss outside. I miss going to the park, the pool, and the zoo. COVID-19 has truly changed everything.

Easton Locken

NORTH DAKOTA

I don't care for COVID-19 for many reasons. I don't get to hang out with my friends as much as I would like to, and I especially miss playing sports and watching them on TV, one of my favorite things to do. We haven't been able to travel as much as a family due to the hot spots in different states and cities, and we also don't get to see as many family members as we would like to.

It's hard to see all the elderly people just hanging out at home because they don't want to venture out in fear of getting the virus. That makes me sad. Masks are so hot and uncomfortable, but I will do anything to keep the spread of the virus to a minimum. Also, I don't like the fact that some of my favorite stores had to close due to COVID-19. I can't wait to go back to school and be in the classroom again. I come from a great state and we are all in this together and we will get through it.

Rahel Tseganeh

WASHINGTON, D.C.

A very important issue that is happening now in my life is COVID-19. I know this is a problem for almost everyone, but the reason that it is so personal to me is that my mom works at a nursing home. She must keep working to support our family, and to care for her patients who need her attention. Nursing homes cannot be shut down and my mom cannot work from home, so she must keep working.

Shortly after the outbreak, my mom became very worried. She was afraid that if she caught the coronavirus, she might pass it on to me (and others), and then I might die. So she sent me to live with different relatives until life is back to normal. Now I miss her so much, and I feel so bad and helpless, even guilty that she cannot just leave her job for a while. At the same time, I am proud of her for helping others.

Everybody wants their old lives back, when people could gather with family and strangers alike without worry, when people did not die from this virus. Now, it's hard for everybody. I am especially sad that so many people are suffering and dying. Families are being broken apart. It's like a crack on a heart and all the love is falling out, and while the world is trying to seal the crack, it cannot do so.

Before this happened, I was focused on myself and pleased for having done well in elementary school. I arrived in this country as a two-year-old immigrant, and now I speak three languages and have earned a scholarship for next year. I'm also a proud American citizen, and so are my mom and uncle.

Now, that all seems selfish and unimportant to me, as I worry about my mom. I am just a fifth grader who cannot leave the house, so what can I do to let others know that this is important in my life? Well, I am writing about it, and that helps. Also, I can provide emotional support and appreciation to my mom. I do call her every night, and tell her that I love her and that I'm proud of her. Maybe when this is over, my family and friends could organize an event to thank health care workers who have worked so hard and sacrificed so much these past weeks. Maybe as an adult, I could become a researcher and try to find cures.

The outcome that I want is for this virus to be over and to have all our family together and healthy. We all need to stay strong because we are all in this crisis together. But we can't give up. If we all stay strong, we can seal that crack in our hearts and bring back joy.

Mason Pham

SYCUAN RESERVATION

When I first heard about COVID, it was from TV. It was on every station, and every adult talked about it like it was going to end the world. It reminded me of zombie apocalypse shows. Everyone got the disease, and the world would stop because everyone was scared. I couldn't help feeling a little scared myself. My school didn't want us to come in anymore. Good thing my grades were already good, so I wasn't worried about what grade my teacher was going to give me. What I was worried about was not being able to see any of my friends anymore. I don't have a lot of friends, but the ones I hung out the most with, I wouldn't be able to see anymore. That made me nervous and unsure what the thing called quarantine was going to be like.

I am Native American and live on the Sycuan reservation. I live near my family members because most of them also live on the rez. However, we don't really have neighbors nearby so it was often quiet and scary during quarantine. Most of my friends have neighborhood kids they can play with. I felt alone and a little scared that things will never be normal again. My parents didn't let me play outside most of the time during quarantine, but that part was fine. I like staying inside. I like to play video games like most kids my age. I like playing games like Fortnite, and streaming my games. So that part was the best part for me. I enjoyed not having to wake up early and get dressed for school. I remained in my pajamas most days and played until my Dad yelled at me to get off. All in all, it wasn't that bad.

I think the worst part of quarantine was that no one was working. How do people make money? Even all my favorite places to eat were closed. I basically ate whatever frozen foods we had left in the freezer. Some of my favorite frozen foods were Hot Pockets and breakfast sandwiches. The more I think about it, it really wasn't that bad. This was a gamer's dream come true: I had food, I could play all day, and I woke up later.

I think the most hurtful thing I saw was my parents wondering when the world would start again. How were we going to get money, and how we were going to get help? People forget about us on the rez. I saw on the news that food was being passed out to other families on other reservations. Where was our food? Where was our help? And where were our Hot Pockets?

Also, my grandma's brother died. It was really strange that we couldn't go to his funeral. We had to watch his services online. I didn't get to say goodbye. It was a difficult time for my whole family. I didn't know what to say to make my parents feel better, I just hugged them. But honestly glad to not have to wear another suit, I had to wear one to my grandma's funeral over Thanksgiving. It was also a hard time for my family, but at least we had each other. With this funeral, no one was around. Once again, I felt alone and unsure what will happen next. I felt unsure if the world will ever start again. I felt unsure if my friends would remember me. I felt unsure if my life would ever get back to normal.

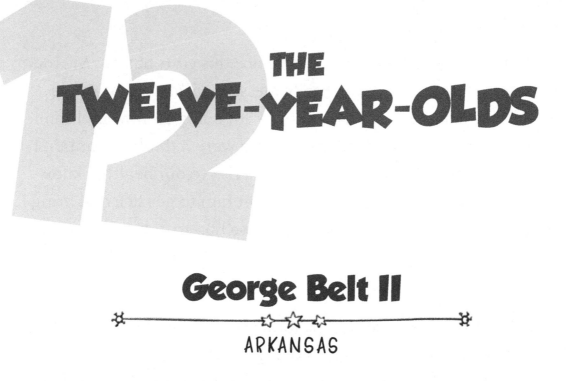

THE Twelve-Year-Olds

George Belt II

ARKANSAS

The infamous COVID-19 came out of nowhere. It seemed like one day we were all normal, then woke up and BAM! Just like that, we had a deadly virus in our world. Yes! The entire world was hit by something I had never heard of and knew nothing about.

This virus has disturbed so many lives, especially mine. I am twelve years old, trying to live my best life being productive in my class and doing whatever. Now I am just sitting away from my friends and only surrounded by my parents and siblings. I cannot go out and do the things that I really want to do. Why? Because nothing is open; my favorite restaurant, the movies, and my favorite stores. This is not how I planned to live in 2020. The only way I could communicate with my friends was with my cell phone and Google Hangouts (so glad my school had Chromebooks.) There was no more in-person interaction. So for me, all I could really do is sit in the house and watch YouTube.

Life in my house has really changed since this virus has hit. My mom works from home and that is really messing with my quarantine social life. She knows everything that I am doing even when I think I am super quiet. My dad still must go to work. I think it is unfair. I feel like since he still goes to work, it is a risk to our health. I know he is being careful, but still I do not want him to get sick and bring it home to us. If we ever went anywhere, we had to put on masks and wipe down the car just for our safety, because we were not taking any chances!

I have been so worried about my family, friends, and their families. I do not think the government is doing what they need to do. They want things back to normal, and that does not ensure the safety of the people. Some people are not even thinking about the amount of people that are dying. They are not wearing masks and do not want to wear them. This is not right, and it makes me wonder if they even care. Another thing is that they should not be so reckless. They know the protocol: if the cases go down in the span of two weeks, then you can reopen. They decided to do it even though the cases are not going down, and people are most likely going to go party and see their friends. That could be the reason there has been a spike in cases. This is not how I planned to live my twelve-year-old life.

I am not enjoying this pandemic, but I feel if we can survive this, we can survive anything. We can learn from this crisis that we are living through, and live a great life.

Tavian Mahin

KENTUCKY

It is weird having to go places and wear masks everywhere. I feel like this will never end. I want things to go back to normal, and to see my friends outside of FaceTime. I want to go back to school and learn regularly. This feels like a never-ending nightmare. All you hear about is more people dying, and more people catching the coronavirus. I want the rest of this year to be normal. This is what I feel like during quarantine.

During quarantine, I have had many fears. One of them is that me and people in my family may die. Another one is that this may be here forever. I have been hanging out with my family, watching movies and swimming in my pool. We have tried to find stuff to do in the house to entertain ourselves. Also, I have done lots of fun stuff like swimming, playing video games, and playing outside. This is what I have been doing during quarantine.

Michaela Alcaraz

HAWAII

When news about a new coronavirus appearing in China spread out to the world, many people seemed very concerned about the virus reaching our state. I think most of us thought we were safe at that time. Boy, were we wrong! Right before spring break, most of us expected things to operate normally. I had no plans to stay home longer than a regular summer break. And yet, here we were! The coronavirus was deemed a pandemic by the WHO soon after it hit home.

Days later, the local news talked about things like the pandemic, the death of George Floyd and the events it set forth, and many other things. It is very ironic how we thought in 2019, this year was going to be a great year, but we get this instead.

Fun fact, while online schooling was still in session, one of my middle school teachers gave us the assignment to keep a diary during the pandemic. Surprisingly, I still do it even though school is already done. There is just one stressful problem. I fall behind schedule with daily entries, and I try to fill it in on different days (but I might resort to skipping days from now on).

Here is something I will never forget from this pandemic. To be clear, nobody in my family has the virus. My dad had surgery on his right knee on Tuesday, July 28th, 2020. Then yesterday, he went to therapy and came home a few hours later. Then it was dinnertime; we ate squid, fish, and rice. He took some medications right after, and sat down to watch some TV. Soon he said his chest was hurting. Mom panicked and asked me to research some solutions for chest pain. We made him drink a cup of warm water and put an ice pack on his chest as he lay down on his bed while Mom called 911. She also told my brother and me to stay outside the house, and make sure our dog Cooper does not bark when help arrives. Moments later, a firetruck came over. The firemen called in an ambulance after coming into the house and asking Dad about the pain. I only knew because I looked through his bedroom window while standing on a chair outside. He then went to the hospital and Mom followed in her car.

My brother and I locked the doors and gates, and we waited three hours for Mom to come home. Later, she came back home with Dad and said everything was fine. It was gastric acid reflux, and it was the food to blame (not the medications). It made us all worried about Dad's safety either way. Times like these can be scary and worrisome, but I know that we will reflect on this time and remember the good that came out of it.

Gerber Rodriguez

CALIFORNIA

So... it has been about three years. Well, that's what it feels like. The point is, people are making it so hard to get out of quarantine so we can just live on with our lives and forget this ever happened.

In the beginning, I told myself I felt free, forgetful, fearless, and fascinated with my family about people's reactions to this crisis. I could just wake up late, and wouldn't have to worry about school that much.

Suddenly, I woke up one day and I felt like I got hit by a million anvils. *Clank! BADABOP! BAM! POW!* That is when the real quarantine started to happen. I had to be subservient, go to my computer, and connect to... an online class. I mean, that sounded cool and all at first. The platform that my future classes were going to be on was a platform called Zoom. "WHAT IS ZOOM?!" I said, plus my connection to the classes were so horrible. Because this very, very bad platform called Zoom came out of nowhere, my connection became some McDonald's Wi-Fi. After the class I saw my beautiful new computer turn into an ugly, elderly math teacher.

Later in this apocalypse, I wanted to buy stuff online. My parents said, "No, that stuff is too expensive." My parents aren't Scrooges or anything, they just wanted the bare necessities like toilet paper and hand sanitizer. Just give me the benefit of the doubt, okay? I was bored, you would do the same too.

So just when I thought nothing could get worse in this pandemic, some "protests" started about abuse of authority, racism, and injustice. Some were also doing illegal protests which included robbery, vandalism, havoc on private property, and everything else that I missed because it's probably on the news right now as we read this. Okay, back to the topic. My life became like a movie, and I was the actor in this movie.

So this is what has happened in my life/movie until now. The good thing about my movie though, is that me, my family, and friends are all safe and sound with toilet paper to spare.

Taylor M. Sheffer

WASHINGTON

I am going into seventh grade, and this is my quarantine school year life. Before school ended, I would wake at 6:00 a.m. and watch YouTube until 8:30 a.m. I would eat breakfast while getting ready for school. Now during the quarantine life, every day I wake at 7:30 a.m. and as soon as I wake up, I eat breakfast. Then I get ready for my Zoom, and this would repeat every day. Monday and Thursday Zoom was reading, math, ELA, and WIN. It was super fun with my friends. On Wednesday the Zoom was with my big class, but I didn't go to that very much. I liked my teacher working with me on Zoom on Monday and Thursday. Only on Friday I didn't have Zoom, but I would go on a bike ride with my family or go swimming, and that's my week for school!

I'm glad it's the summer and my family put up our pool. My brother got a new dog (it's a husky). His name is Boeau, he is super cute.

My sister is a year older, and she didn't have as much fun with quarantine school. They didn't have any Zoom classes to teach her anything. I am glad I had such a great teacher.

So that's my quarantine school!

Sydnee May

UTAH

My experience with COVID-19 has been very interesting, to say the least.

I was a typical sixth-grader at a local charter school, and wasn't very put off by the coronavirus, as I had only heard bits and pieces from my teachers, fellow students, and my parents. All I knew was that there was a bad disease in some far off countries, and with my own problems that I was dealing with, why should I worry about something that didn't affect me?

But that soon started to change. I went to school one Friday morning (March 13th) after learning that COVID had started to close schools, and that our school was possibly getting closed, depending on a meeting that was happening later that day. I talked about that with my friends that day, and soon they had convinced me that it wouldn't happen. I finished my day and went home. My mom sat down at her laptop and went online. I had a snack and commenced on my homework, when I heard a gasp from my mom.

I rushed over to her and looked at her screen to see that the governor of Utah had announced a "soft closure" for the next two weeks. I gasped. I had seen my friends for the last time for two weeks, and as I later learned, the next few months.

You see, I'm a member of a high-risk family. My dad has diabetes, which means that he is especially at-risk of getting especially sick or dying from COVID. That also means that I have to stay at home when a lot of other people can go to places.

I proceeded to do online school for the next two months until school was over. If my city is still in the yellow zone by the beginning of school, then we will either do online school or go to school with masks.

Due to social distancing, I have not seen my friends face-to-face in two to three months. We still talk to each other over video calls and over the phone, but it is not the same.

Looking back on life before coronavirus, I wish I had complained less, enjoyed life more, and been more thankful for every day that I got to go to school. I would've spent more time outside, and around people.

I have missed out on so many events. Some people try to make it so I can come, but it's worth staying at home to protect my dad.

While these times have been crazy, they have also brought out the best in us. They have been an opportunity for me to grow closer to my family and friends, and I am thankful for that.

Isabela Charriez

NEW JERSEY

I am quarantined with two sisters, one brother, my parents, and my dog. As you can imagine, it can be a little chaotic in my house. With so many people, you might think that we never get bored because we can just play with each other. That is not exactly true. My brother, who is fourteen, just wants to stay in his room all day. My younger sisters want to play with dolls and do cheerleading. I love playing with my siblings, but it is hard to decide what to play. Do not get me started on movies and shows. It is so hard to pick something that we all enjoy. I like watching nature shows, my brother likes Marvel, and my sisters like princesses and Disney. It is hard to agree on movies in my house. But there is something that has really helped me get through this pandemic: I love to write devotions.

Writing is a way for me to express how I feel and how I interpret things. I am shy and quiet, but reading God's word encourages me to help people. I share my devotions with my family and some people at my church. But it is not by my own power. The Holy Spirit leads me and guides me to write. One of my favorite devotions that I have been led to write is from Numbers 20:2-5. This was when the Israelites were in the desert. I really like this passage because right now we are going through a desert of our own.

The Israelites were traveling through the desert to the promised land. Many of them complained that they had no water or food. Some wished to die. Some even wanted to go back to Egypt. They did not trust God, but God brought them through the desert. When we feel like giving up, just remember that God is always there for you. Trusting God will get us through tough times. Right now, we are all going through a desert. Not one filled with sand, but one that feels like you cannot see where it ends. A worldwide pandemic, racial inequalities, disagreements, riots, an economic crisis, and people dying. These are things that seem like they will never stop. People just want to give up. They are scared about what is going to happen.

Adults, teenagers, and kids are all worried and confused. Times right now are uncertain. But there is one thing that we can always trust and depend on, God's word and praying. God knows exactly what is going to happen. He is that only one that can stop COVID-19, racism, people dying, and all our problems. We need to know Jesus and have a relationship with Him so we can have hope. He will bring us through this.

Jaydin R. Chong

NEW YORK

When I first heard about COVID-19, I never thought it was going to change our lives the way it did. It seems like it all happened so fast, from one day to the next, things were completely different. It felt like we were living in a different world, or in a different time zone. For starters, I never thought I wasn't going to be able to go back to school or see my friends and teachers again for the rest of my sixth grade year. I was excited at first because I felt I needed a break from school, so I convinced myself it was a surprise mini-vacation. But then, I started realizing it might be longer than we thought. So I knew I had to adapt to this new way of learning, which for me was not the greatest. I enjoy being in a classroom setting with my teachers guiding and helping us with our work, and seeing my classmates learn and sometimes goof around. I just missed how things were. At first I was doing good and keeping up, but honestly I started getting lazy and comfortable. My sleep schedule changed and I just couldn't sleep. Every night I went to sleep a little later and later. It wasn't that I didn't have a bed time, I just couldn't sleep sometimes. So when my mom would wake me up to start my day, I would be so tired and cranky. I was having a hard time concentrating and putting my all into my work. My mom would keep up with my grades through an app my school has, and boy she was not so happy with me when she seen those grades. I even got punished a couple times, I wasn't allowed to play video games or have my phone until I pulled up my grades. It was annoying, but I know that she had to do what she thought was best. That made me really sad though, because I was thankful that due to technology I was able to keep in touch with my friends. We were able to still talk to each other on FaceTime, and while we played video games together in a group. It honestly became our daily routine, so when that was taken away from me, I really felt it. Again, I know that if my mom didn't push me to do better, and even punish me when she did, I would not have ended my year too well. With motivation and support from my mom, family, and friends, I was able to make up some missing assignments, keep up with my new assignments, and I managed to finish the year with a B- average. It isn't the best I could have done, but I do appreciate my mom for understanding that it wasn't easy and for doing everything she could to support me when I was having a difficult time. I realized through the pandemic more than ever before that there was nothing I had to do alone in this world, as long as I had my mom and family by my side and also my good friends. Most of my friends and I have been raised together, or known each other since kindergarten. Although we like to have fun, play video games, and do normal teen stuff, I'm happy that we all know school is important too. We all have our own skills or passion, and as long as we support each other and be there for each other we can be friends during and after this pandemic and hopefully forever. Lastly, I really hope that in the fall we'll be able to go back to school and have fun again. But if we can't because it's not safe, then at least I know what I have to do and still create a good experience while learning from home, with my support system by my side.

Joshua Jason

LOUISIANA

March 13th, 2020 started off as just another day, but little did I know it would be a game-changer. As I sat in science class reviewing last week's test, my teacher began to speak off-topic: "Class, due to the coronavirus outbreak, school will be closed for two weeks and we will return in April once everything is under control." In complete shock at what I had just heard, I gathered my belongings with the hopes of returning in two weeks. This was the beginning of my corona experience.

I love everything about school, especially math class. Multiplication, fractions, and division are my favorite parts of math class. Learning at home started out great, my parents are very supportive and hands-on when it comes to education. I have two younger siblings who I would help with assignments, in between completing my work. It was fun to show off my math skills while helping them.

The best thing about my corona experience was having my entire family home on a daily basis. My dad is a truck driver and spends most of his time on the road, so having him home was really fun. We had movie nights, family time, and bible study during quarantine. The thing I didn't like most about quarantine was not having baseball due to COVID-19. Later on, I found out baseball was reopening due to COVID-19 break. I wanted to work even harder, considering we only had three tournaments left. My corona break had ups and downs, but overall I learned that my family is the most important thing in my life.

CyZariah Jones

MISSISSIPPI

It all started the day before spring break. My class had a party with ice cream and cookies, and we watched a movie to celebrate spring break. I had a lot of fun, but little did I know that it was going to be the last day of school. So I said goodbye to my teachers and friends, and said I was going to see them in a week. In the middle of the week, the school district sent out an announcement saying that they were going to take one or two days to sanitize the school because of the coronavirus. That one or two days turned to a week, then a month, and then till the next school year.

When they told me that we didn't have to go to school, I was happy at first because I didn't like to go to school. I mean, what kid likes going to school? But as the days went by, I was tired of being at home and acting like every day is Saturday. I missed school. I missed talking to my friends and laughing at the class clown's jokes. It's not the same talking on the phone.

If you don't know what coronavirus is, it is a disease that originated from China. It goes by many names, coronavirus, COVID-19, "Rona," and "Corona." The most common symptoms of the coronavirus are a fever, dry cough, and the feeling of tiredness. You also have to take a number of precautions to keep safe. Some of those precautions are wearing a mask that covers both your nose and mouth when you are going places, and washing your hands at least for twenty seconds. They made us stay in quarantine. We couldn't go anywhere or be in a place with more than ten people.

It sounds kind of bad, but it's also a good thing because it gives you a lot of time to spend with your family. At the beginning of quarantine my dad had to work from home, and because of that he wasn't too busy to watch a movie or go to the store. In my opinion, I think this is God telling us to never take something for granted, because I didn't like or miss school until I stopped going.

For most of June last year, I went to this university program. This year I got accepted again. It's two programs in one, called the GEMS program because we're diamonds in the rough. There's the STEM Changers program, for sixth to eighth grade, and there's the Bridge program, for high schoolers. I'm in the STEM program. STEM stands for Science, Technology, Engineering, and Math. Last year we went on two trips. We also ate in the university cafeteria, walked on campus, and learned more stuff for the next school year. They also paid us at the end of the program, and rewarded us for our hard work in the classes. This all goes back to the coronavirus, because this year we didn't get to go on any trips, eat in the cafeteria, or even go on campus. This year we did the program virtually, on the Zoom app. It was fun but it wasn't the same as being on campus.

So as you can see, coronavirus has made a big impact on my life but it has also helped me. It taught me how to appreciate something when you have it and enjoy it. Yes, I missed some opportunities or moments in my life, but it also helped me to get closer to my family. That is my corona experience.

DeVaughn Holmes

ALABAMA

When COVID-19 appeared I wasn't concerned because of there being very few cases, but as the cases began to escalate and schools were shutting down, I became more concerned. At the time, all I could think about was "how long are we out?", "how will we be educated?", because at the time we were still in school. COVID-19 had an impact on my everyday life because I had to start thinking of ways to fill the eight hour school day void. Usually I would come home at 2:30 or so, and eat, do homework, get my game time, and watch TV. COVID-19 escalated slowly. It shut my school down, changing my life tremendously.

So we are now four months into this pandemic. I have passed the sixth grade as an honor student with A's, and the school system is straightened out for the time being. As of today, I have found things to do with my day. I draw, read my Bible, have an hour of education, take a walk in my neighborhood, gaming (of course), and I've even found myself working for my principal who lives across the street. I have developed a new everyday life, including multiple activities. Each day I am discovering more things to do with my time.

I am glad no one in my immediate family has come down with or lost their life to COVID-19; with the exception of my great-uncle who was eighty-two years old. Not only has no one come down with it, but also my family has not shown any signs of symptoms. I'm especially thankful since a lot of people in my family go out, but they are careful to social distance. We go places like restaurants, parks, visit close family, the grocery store, and other essential places. I am thankful for the well-being of my family.

When the pandemic is over I look forward to going back to school, getting back into my social life, and always stimulating my mind five days a week at school. Furthermore, I look forward to being able to go anywhere with anyone. The things I will miss are sleeping in, staying up later than usual, and less school work.

My COVID-19 experience has been like a roller coaster ride that progressed from my life when COVID-19 hit, to how I adapted through the last four months, to the outcome on others around me, including friends and family during COVID-19. Some of my COVID-19 experience has been unfortunate, but some has been amazing.

Abigail Curry

COLORADO

When quarantine first started, I was really upset because this was my sixth-grade year and I was super excited for events like my spring orchestra concert and the spring musical. I was so excited to be on stage and perform, then COVID struck. When the cast of the musical was told over Zoom that we wouldn't perform, I was so upset and angry. Not only was I one of the few sixth graders cast, it was also our drama teacher's last year before retirement, so you could say I was pretty bummed. When I heard that we had to do remote learning for the rest of the year, I was so mad because who wants to learn over a computer screen? Especially when you're a physical learner like me, I knew it was going to be hard. I struggled so much I almost didn't pass the grade, but thank God my mom and dad were there to help me get my work in.

After school ended, I was bored because all I had was TV to watch. My mom and dad were working all the time and with five siblings, I got pretty annoyed fast. One thing that affected me a lot was not being able to go to church and interact with my church family. Luckily, they did online service that me and my family attended every Sunday morning. As the middle child in the family, I had to figure out how to keep myself busy, so I started to cook a lot of food. I made soup, lasagna, and even a full course meal! Cooking is something I love to do, but never had time for before, so I was happy.

Soon enough Fourth of July came around, which is one of my favorite holidays. On Fourth of July, we have a big feast with all sorts of delicious treats. I even got to make yummy cupcakes with red, white, and blue frosting. That day was so awesome, at the time COVID had eased up a little, so my mom let us go shopping with her. Of course, there was an extensive sanitization process as soon as we got home, we had to take showers and all that jazz. Now it's August; I go back to school in two days, and I'm gonna start my seventh-grade year off great.

Thomas D. Grady IV

ILLINOIS

The coronavirus pandemic, also known as COVID-19, has affected us all in many ways. Health officials have advised us to isolate from others, and people have lost their jobs and their lives, causing fear to traverse the globe. While I know the virus will affect my future, I am unable to determine exactly how. We can speculate, but everything is still so uncertain. This virus is spreading like gossip in a schoolhouse. Based on Channel 7's research, if you follow social distancing rules, you minimize the chance of contracting COVID-19 to approximately 10%. I fear that some members of certain factions will not act responsibly to contain and reduce the spread of the virus. That's why prayer becomes important. There is no way of knowing what will happen, so I choose to put my trust in God.

There are twenty-three companies in Northern America competing to create a vaccine. These companies are just racing for the dollar, looking to profit from this situation. In hopes of finding a cure, the drug companies are asking for guinea pigs or anyone willing to be a test subject. I assume most of them have passed away, because chemists, scientists, and doctors haven't found a vaccine. So our future is in their hands, to find a cure and bring an end to COVID-19. This pandemic won't just affect my future, it also affects my friends' and loved ones' futures as well.

I find it difficult to deal with the virus because we have been asked to stay home to stop the spread of the infection. Before COVID-19, as a society we were able to travel freely, attend family gatherings, public sporting events, graduations, and just do our everyday routines. Now instead, we have all learned to communicate with technology. For example, we use Zoom, Google Meet, and other apps to do things virtually. I try to salvage something positive from these uncertain times. Staying home allows time to find out who we really are and build our relationship with family, while taking a break from the catastrophes.

I have several things that I have thought about and questioned. Several states are reopening in phases, will people be safe? Will our economy recover from this? If so, then how? Will we really be able to rebuild successfully? What prevents the virus from reoccurring? Why weren't we prepared this time? Will my childhood have to be disrupted again? What does the future look like for my family and me?

We will remain hopeful; we will pray and wait on a vaccine while staying at least six feet apart.

THE THIRTEEN-YEAR-OLDS

Dominic Hall

KANSAS

Man, oh man! COVID-19 came in like a deer in headlights. Just when I was doing pretty good, here comes Mr. Covid. I had amazing grades and was completing my last few months as a middle school student. I had so much planned; college visits, high school tours, and track season was officially beginning. Then, here comes this coronavirus to end all of my middle school end of the school year events. I was heartbroken. Everything was ruined; the dances, yearbook signing parties, awards ceremonies, year-end gatherings, and promotion to high school ceremony. Needless to say, I was crushed. I had made so many friends and God knows when I will get to see them again. When this COVID thing first came to our country, I was unimaginably sad. I couldn't go anywhere, I couldn't see my classmates. The media started reporting about this horrible virus all over the country and world. It was so much negativity about it all. At first, I really thought the world was going to end. I tried my best not to think about it all.

I'm only thirteen years old, hopefully this is not it. I don't want my life to end here. I have been taught by my youth leaders and pastor to have faith in God no matter the circumstance. Although people are dying and unemployment is at an all-time high, my relationship with the Lord is getting closer and closer every day. I understand the importance of taking care of others and praying for other people. I started focusing on improving my life. I work out every day. I actually lost some much needed weight, which is incredible to me. I also work on my academics some, and am preparing for the upcoming school year, if we have it. I really believe the virus could be slowed down, but our national leadership needs to improve the way it responds to this pandemic. I rarely leave the house, but I try and venture out some. I trust God according to the proverb in the Bible: "Trust in the Lord and lean not unto your own understanding." I know through all this, God will bring us out and he definitely has a plan for me.

Levi Pufahl

MONTANA

Living in COVID has sure been an experience. I live with my two sisters and our two parents. Our parents have been really confusing. On one hand, they say everything is going to be fine and we're going to be alright. On the other hand, they tell us "we've never experienced anything like this before" and "anything could happen." So living in COVID has *definitely* been an experience.

School just got out, so let's talk about that: I like to think that the school year is split into fourths. The COVID part of the year was ¾ of the year. If I could describe virtual schooling with one word, it would be "stressful." That is not against the teachers in any way! The fact that their bosses basically said, "we are not going back to school and you have a week to figure this online teaching stuff out" is crazy! And by the end of the year my teachers made it work, which is mind-blowing!

Although there's not many, one upside to COVID is we got a puppy and he is just adorable! COVID has been a really confusing and frankly scary time. But I do think that we as Americans, as a people, and as a culture will survive this. America will not turn into a post-apocalyptic barren landscape like some people who over-exaggerate think it is going to become.

Sage Nicholson

OREGON

Ballet is my passion. The feeling I get when I dance is like no other. Dance is pure joy in my mind. The studio is my second home and whatever is going on outside, good or bad, melts away. The teachers at my studio, especially our director, are some of the most incredible people I have ever met. They inspire us to be our best each day, have huge hearts, a passion for dance, and a desire to include everyone and make it accessible to all. I hope that one day I can be half as inspirational as they are.

Realizing that quarantine was going to be a while, they immediately jumped to virtual and held classes online the week after quarantine started. They even found a way for us to perform our spring show virtually! Nonetheless, dancing in a pandemic... is hard. You have the time and opportunity to work hard and become better, but find yourself being lazy and unmotivated, trying to dance in a tiny space by yourself, staring at your classmates and teachers on a computer screen.

Being super careful and diligent about taking care of our health has been a huge endeavor. We have all had to adjust to working, teaching, and learning from home. That has been hard for some, and not so hard for others. For myself, being a social person in quarantine has been hard, but Zoom calls have been my saving grace. It is a great way for me to be social without a mask, gloves, hand sanitizer, or social distancing.

We have no health care or essential workers in our family, and nobody close to me has gotten COVID. My life has only slowed down, and we've had to get creative on how we navigate the store, connecting with others safely and from a distance.

They say write what you know, write from the heart. Other people have lost family, friends, jobs, grandparents, freedoms, health, and so much more. I can't write about that, because I have been blessed with the people I love continuing to be healthy, but I can extend my heartache and prayers for others as they grieve their losses.

There have been some very unfortunate things going on during this pandemic, and I wish that the world would take a second look at what it was doing as we mourn the death of those who have passed.

I wish we would stand up for what is right, find peace with each other, and share what we have learned, so that together we can find a vaccine and quickly produce and share it with each other. We need each other. The world is just one big community, and we need to work together to take care of it.

My take-away from quarantine is to be grateful for all my blessings during this scary time; and to pray for our world, our leadership, and us, coming together, letting nothing stand in our way to beat this pandemic. We will rise in the face of adversity. But who knows how the Lord will aid our endeavors, time will only tell.

Somiyah Harding

WEST VIRGINIA

The COVID-19 pandemic has been difficult, but we have been blessed. Many people were without basic necessities, including food, but we had everything that we needed. Many people lost their jobs, or their jobs were affected. My mom's job was affected too, but she was able to continue working from home. Many people lost family members to the virus, but our family was spared from losing anyone.

I was sad at first, because I couldn't see my friends, and finish my school year with them. Our school was beginning tryouts for spring sports when the crisis hit our town, so spring sports were not held. Our All-County choir rehearsals, competitions, and concert were cancelled. I was looking forward to sports tryouts, choir concerts, and "moving up" day at school.

I have four younger siblings, and we all had to be home-schooled. My mom split her work hours up, and between meetings, she home-schooled us. We took turns on the computer, laptop and tablets to complete our homework and assignments. My brother, Jeremiah (who is eleven), and I helped our younger siblings if they needed it. My mom took a lot of time with us to make sure that we were doing our homework, even though she had to work too. My siblings and I came out with very good grades, and I think home-schooling was easier for me, because I had one-on-one help when I needed it.

Being at home all the time was sometimes stressful, but it was fun being at home. We live in a rural area, so we were always able to go outside and spend time doing things together. My mom, brother, and I would check on our neighbors and church members, and we shopped for them so they didn't have to go out.

My heart hurts for all of the families that have lost family members. I pray for the healthcare workers who are sacrificing their lives and working tirelessly for others. I pray for the leaders of our nation and those who are in authority, that they make the right decisions. I pray that God continues to bless and protect His people.

Luke and Noah Nelsen

MAINE

Luke:

COVID-19 has been bad for everybody, including me. We haven't seen anything like this in over 100 years, and for me online school has not been fun.

Personally, I haven't had anyone that I know die from COVID, but I see all over the news people dying and I think it's just horrible. It has also been hard not to stretch my legs and go to any place majorly populated, but you got to do what you got to do. But there have been a few bright sides to this horrible situation. For example, I spend much more time with my family and go camping a lot more now, and I know that our planet is getting a break from all the pollution since the COVID-19 pandemic started. Other than that, COVID-19 has been a horrible situation for everybody, but we are trying to make the best of it.

Another reason COVID-19 has been a struggle is that nobody has seen something like this in over 100 years, since the outbreak of the Spanish flu virus. In my lifetime I've never heard of a pandemic like this, and when it started I had no idea how it would turn out. When I first heard about COVID-19 like anybody I wasn't very worried, because I heard it was in China, far from the USA. But when it came to the USA, I did not know what was going to happen. Now that it's been over four months I've started to relax, but when quarantine first started it was scary. But that is why it was a freak-out to me and most people, because nobody has seen something like this in forever.

The third way that COVID-19 has affected me personally is that online school has not been the best. For example, in my school we had a pass-fail grade, which basically means if you did the assignment you pass, but if you didn't you failed. The problem with that is they gave us many assignments, and it was very hard to keep up with all of them. It's also been hard for me because some of the information we were given in this work was not taught to us before the outbreak hit. It is hard for me to learn online because when we are at school we are in a work environment, but when we are at home we are not. It is not as tough for everyone, but I just found it very tough. I know others have it worse, but it has also been a stressful time for me and for everybody else. I hope our country can get through this okay, even if I think we aren't handling this pandemic very well.

Noah:

2020 has been a record-setting year, and it will go down as one of the strangest years ever in history. We have never seen anything like this, in this generation or generations before us. For me, school has been pretty bad so far because of the online part. I have not been able to see any of my family and friends except through texting and FaceTime. Online school is bad just because it's been very hard for the teachers to teach, and it's been pretty easy to cheat or just go on your phone the whole time it's happening. The teachers haven't been communicating to us very well and expect us just to figure it out on our own, but I guess it's probably hard for them too. I usually get to see my family and friends over the summer but I haven't because my parents are very worried about the coronavirus. So the summer has been pretty fun, but it's been long and some parts of it blew. Hopefully I'll get to see my family soon. Another way it has impacted me is just seeing the news and seeing how many people have died. I just think, "Wow, this is actually pretty serious." Just thinking, "Wow this has killed so many people, are we next?" Hopefully not. There have been a few positives, but there have been a lot of negatives about 2020.

Michia-Marie Ward

WISCONSIN

COVID-19: the only thing I have heard the past few months. Rising case numbers, how to stay safe, everywhere I look, it is surrounding me. I have had to adjust a lot. Learning from home, watching my father out on the front lines, even keeping myself healthy. I think that at the end of this, we will all come out stronger on the other side because we have learned how to support and care for each other. The living situation of today does not make it any easier, having to stay inside all cramped up in your house. Coronavirus has taken not only a physical toll on me personally, but a mental one as well. Welcome to a child's mind through a pandemic.

Boring: technically defined as not interesting, tedious, according to Merriam Webster's dictionary. In my words, eight long hours filled with work, work, and even more work. Learning from home honestly has been a new experience, and I cannot say whether it was good or bad, it was somewhere in between. I am personally a kinesthetic learner, which means that I need to be hands-on to retain information. Virtual learning takes away every part of that. I prefer to be in the classroom with a real teacher, real children, and real work in front of me when learning, and so having to do everything online kind of messed me up. I felt my grades at the end of the year beginning to slip from me just not being able to focus or deeply learn any information. I feel that the whole learning from home was just not the best idea and that learners like me were not considered when the idea was conceived.

And secondly, my health. I am not a person who likes to express emotion. I do not talk to a therapist or anything like that, I usually just do things to busy myself. So when I am stuck inside, I am sure you can imagine how hard it is for me to find things to do, so that I can distract myself. During this time, stress has been one of the biggest things that I have seen rising in myself, and so I began to practice yoga and breathing techniques to help relieve stress and relax. Writing poetry is also good for me because I can express my emotions and label them. Physical health is also a really big thing, because I know that most of the time I'm either sleeping or eating. So getting out and going on walks is really important, not only for your body but for your mind so you don't get cabin fever.

Overall, I think that this time has given everyone a lot of opportunities to branch out to people we do not get to see often, and given us time with our loved ones. We have refashioned our minds to find new ways to connect and be together even when we cannot really be together.

Travon Pemberton

CONNECTICUT

Dealing with the COVID-19 virus has been very stressful. At the beginning, I didn't think the virus was that bad, then people started dying and the virus started spreading. Now literally it has spread all around the world. Everything is different now; I must stay inside, and I am not able to go to school or see my friends.

I still see some of my friends on FaceTime, or I talk to them through my video games, however it's not the same. Each day after school we would go to the park, and play basketball or a game called "Man Hunt." Man Hunt is like hide-and-seek, but you play at night. It's fun, and I miss doing that with my friends. Since the pandemic, all the parks have been closed. We are forced to stay inside or if we do go outside, we must wear protective coverings such as a mask and gloves.

During this pandemic, I am grateful that I get to spend more time with my family. I am also able to help my community, and give them food. I would never have the time to volunteer if we were not at home because of the virus. I did not think that I would enjoy it as much as I do.

I volunteer with a program called Foodshare. Foodshare is the regional food bank in Connecticut that provides emergency distribution of food for the entire state. During this period, there are so many people that don't have enough food. I am one of the youngest volunteers currently participating in the program. I really like volunteering and working there because I enjoy helping others. I also like the fact that I can meet other people and make new friends.

I wear a mask and gloves when I volunteer, and even though it's uncomfortable and at times hot, I still wear it. Wearing a mask helps to keep everyone safe and stops the spreading of the virus. My grandmother and grandfather recently had surgery, so we don't go out without protecting ourselves because we don't want to bring anything around them and cause them to get sick.

I hope that I can be an example to other kids my age. I want to inspire them to volunteer as well. I want them to know that they can do something and make a difference.

LibbyAnn Latimore

IOWA

"Words cannot express my gratitude. All that I am and ever hope to be, I owe it all to you." ~ To God Be the Glory, Kelly Price

Death is a thing that is unexplainable. When you go through death, it triggers things from your past and brings them to the present. Losing your loved ones takes a toll on you, your family, and changes your life. This is how it changed mine. These past couple months, things in my life have been spiraling down. My family members have been in the hospital, and I have had two deaths in the past year from February to June 20th. I haven't had a break, my emotions have been spiraling out of control. Being thirteen and not knowing what to do when someone you love is gone is sickening; you can't understand what you're feeling, but you know it's normal to feel the way you do. When my aunts died, I cried because I was very close to them. They say it takes a village to raise a child; village members are gone, they will never return, and it hurts. I feel like they left me too soon. They were amazing, there was never a dull moment with them when they would walk into a room and light it up. Both had so much to give in such little time. On February 3rd, we got a call from my uncle saying that my aunt had been murdered. My mom bought a ticket and flew to Kokomo, Indiana. A few weeks after, my father and my sister, along with my nieces and nephews, drove eight hours to bury my aunt. My grandmother preached her funeral. Months flew by, and the killer was still in question. On June 5th, we finally found her killer and she was served justice. In March my school closed down due to COVID-19, we then went on spring break, and after started virtual learning. It was a challenge for me to adapt to virtual learning. At first I worked on school a lot and accomplished lots of things while doing so, but towards the end of the school year is when I started to fall off the wagon. I slacked because that's when I wasn't able to comprehend my schoolwork. I asked for help, but wasn't getting as much clarification as I needed. I bounced back as hard as I could, and passed all of my classes with good grades. COVID-19 drastically changed my life. At the beginning of virtual learning I struggled, because I couldn't understand the curriculum being taught to me. But with persistent parents pushing me to achieve any goal I set for myself, I accomplished everything I wanted to this year.

Spring break was around the time my parents had contracted COVID-19. We went as a family to Kansas City to go to church;

someone there had COVID-19, and my parents and church members contracted it. My parents came back to Iowa and laid in bed miserable. My sister-in-law came and nursed my parents back to health, and we overcame the trick of the enemy. We thought that was the end, but it was only the beginning. My grandfather had prostate cancer for months; we waited for surgery, but because of COVID-19 it was constantly postponed. Before my grandfather went for surgery he had to get a COVID-19 test. He came back negative, so to the doctors that was a "go" for surgery. Once my grandfather was out of surgery, we talked to him and he seemed fine. The doctors said that after a few more days, he could be released. Unfortunately, he contracted COVID-19 while in the hospital. My grandfather remained in the hospital for three weeks; while he was there he coded twice, but regained his strength back and made a perfect recovery. A couple weeks later, another thing was thrown at me. My aunt recently had gotten fired, but wanted to maintain a steady income, so she decided to get another job at a temp agency. In the middle of her training she began to get sick, and came to find out a person at the agency knowingly had COVID-19. My aunt tried to get a free test, but got turned away by the state of Iowa multiple times for various reasons. At that point she quarantined herself for two weeks. She brought home COVID-19, my oxygen-dependent grandmother contracted COVID-19, and it hit both of my family members hard. Closer to the end of the week they were both admitted to the hospital. In the hospital my aunt and grandmother were getting worse by the minute, they both coded multiple times. The doctors described it as a spiritual connection between the two (at the time the doctor and nurse didn't understand that they were mother and daughter), he also said that it was like they were talking to each other spiritually, saying "You go, I'll stay." While these things were happening, they were on the ventilators. We Zoomed with them every day to see their condition. Gradually my grandmother started making progress, she started to open her eyes and slowly regained her strength. My aunt, on the other hand, wasn't making any progress and coded three times. My family made the decision to take her off the ventilator, and not a second later she rolled her eyes to the back of her head and died. Within a week we had a homegoing service and her body was cremated. Now she is in the living room with a glass case and her remains are with us every day. My grandmother came home and had to bear the weight of losing a child and the weight of staying healthy: she came out of the hospital still oxygen-dependent but also an insulin-dependent person.

Sadness is what I feel life has been hitting me with, one thing after another. I feel like a building that keeps getting hit by wrecking balls. The reason I'm sad is because my family is missing people to make our circle whole. I feel bad for those who never got to know those amazing women that I lost. I feel bad for those who never said sorry for the things that they did to them. One thing I can say is that time is borrowed. My aunties had so little time to do so much work, but I believe they accomplished everything they needed to in their years of living, and poured out everything God instilled in them. Overall, this year has been a roller coaster for me and my family, but no matter what was brought to me, I prayed and fasted and stayed with God. Throughout this rough journey, I feel like things are going to turn around for good, but one thing that always works is prayer.

Anna Sinclaire Cooper

MICHIGAN

Before this pandemic, I was living my best life. A month and a half before the lockdown, my cheer team and I were in Florida, at Universal Studios, after winning first place in our cheerleading competition. My eighth grade class had decided to go to Niagara Falls in Canada for spring break. I began trying on formal spring dresses for our eighth grade banquet. Plans were in motion. Three days before a significant cheer competition, the quarantine went into effect.

Rumors about the disease began to spread faster than the disease itself. One of the many assumptions was that black people could not catch COVID-19. Another story was that kids were immune. I knew it was serious when all school activities were suspended for the remainder of the school year. No more movies, malls were closed, no school trips, no dance, no graduation ceremony, and unbelievably, face-to-face church service was discontinued.

For the first time in my life, I didn't want to leave the house. For at least sixty days of quarantine, I was afraid that someone I loved would contract the virus and die. As the number of people dying and getting sick increased, with no cure in sight, I felt hopeless.

Coronavirus drastically affected my life. Not being able to go school for face-to-face learning and socializing with my friends has spoiled my school year. I did not like virtual learning. I couldn't see my family, especially my grandma in the nursing home. My other grandma's birthday was a drive-by party where we stood outside on her lawn. For my birthday we ordered take-out from Red Lobster, and celebrated virtually with my cousins and friends.

This quarantine allowed me to learn how to cook on my own, bake cookies from scratch, and exercise while singing and dancing on TikTok. Best of all, my parents allowed us to get a dog. Most recently, I decided to start a graphic t-shirt business called Sinclaire Beauty Collection. Taking care of a new dog and always filling t-shirt orders has kept me busy and safely occupied.

As Governor Gretchen slowly opens the State of Michigan, my family and I have ventured out. My siblings and I have gone bike riding, and to the beach. We have walked our dogs on the Riverwalk in downtown Detroit. I continue to practice social distancing, and wear a mask whenever in public. In conclusion, this pandemic has caused me to miss out on many milestones, but I would rather keep my family and friends healthy and alive than sick and dying. Meanwhile, I hope and pray that things get better.

Ricayla Lemonias

ARIZONA

It was the first week of my spring break when news broke of the coronavirus outbreak in Wuhan, China. Spreading across the world in a frenzy, it took the lives of many people young and old. It seems like days later, the Governor of Arizona announced the state was under lockdown, including my church and my school. I was overjoyed to get another week off school. I did not understand the impact this was going to make in my life.

COVID-19 presented new challenges for myself and my family. My mother and father, who both work in healthcare, were no longer just our parents. They were our teachers, doctors, our friends, and quite frankly our go-to-persons for everything. I realized then and there that I took for granted the power of social interaction.

School was no longer the same. My brother Jarique and I had to endure online learning and all its complications. At night I could see how tired and frustrated my mother was after a full day at work, but was still determined to see to it that all our assignments were on time. Sometimes I felt like giving up, but I knew that a junior high diploma would be worth it.

My eighth grade graduation was bittersweet. Not being able to see my friends as I received my certificate was saddening, and I was anticipating seeing them receive theirs as well. Still, I got to see my teachers and thank them for what they had done to help me.

COVID-19 also affected my ability to go to church, to see my friends and close relatives. I reminisced about our Sunday School and our developing youth program. I really do miss them.

My diet is unbalanced and my sleep schedule is also affected; I fall asleep early and wake up very late. Many worrying things have happened so far, and we are only seven months into the year. Many predict that it will only get worse. Still, I am confident that these times will come to an end someday. It is best to focus less on the negative things at this point. Positivity is key right now, because where there is darkness, God will bring light.

I enjoyed spending more time with my family, and having more time to think about what I want to accomplish in my school life. As for me, I believe that my family somehow became closer with each other, even when apart. Though death has been the center of this pandemic, I truly believe as a young girl, this pandemic has opened my eyes to the ups and down that life has to offer. I believe this experience has truly helped me to become a better person.

Max Leland

NEBRASKA

March 13th, 2020: my thirteenth birthday. I never would have known that would be the last day of semi-normalcy for four months and counting. Our school district canceled school, so we thought we were just getting an extra day for spring break. Then spring break came and we didn't go back to school... for the rest of the year. See at first, it was just my birthday party that was canceled. And then my birthday trip. Then my sister's sixteenth birthday party was canceled. And then my other sister's eighteenth birthday. She also had her prom, graduation, and all senior events cancelled. She's now preparing for college, and who knows what that is going to entail. She and my parents are going through virtual orientation for now, but we really aren't sure what her freshman year of college is going to look like.

My life has been affected by COVID-19 in many ways. At first, it was cool. I was able to go to school in my pajamas, binge-watch shows on Netflix, and master games on my Switch. But then it started to get real. Immediately, our family stocked up on food and necessities. My mom was the only one to leave the house, and only for essentials. We ordered everything else to be delivered--food, groceries, and household essentials. My parents turned our house into a school and office building for all five of us. Day in and day out, my parents both worked and my sisters and I did our schoolwork from home. Then we would take a drive on the weekends to get out of the house. When this all started, it was still cold and rainy in Omaha. As the weather turned, we were able to get out and go on walks with our dogs, ride our bike, etc. Shortly after school ended, the direct impacts hit. Both of my sisters lost their jobs -- one was a lifeguard and one was a busser at a restaurant. Then my stepdad lost his job. After six weeks, he was able to find a new job, and now has to go into his office location every day. They have virtually no COVID-19 precautions. Nobody in his office wears a mask and social distancing is not a requirement.

My extended family was significantly impacted as well. One of my aunts is an OB/GYN and was working extra shifts at the hospital. Every day she risked exposure, and had to take a lot of extra precautions with my uncle and cousin. Another uncle works for a car dealership and was effectively out of his job until they were able to negotiate with the governor to allow for contactless car sales. His wife, my aunt, was considered essential services. She works for an HVAC company and was able to work from home, but returned to work as soon as the Directed Health Measures for Colorado was lifted.

My other aunt wasn't quite as lucky. She worked for a company that provides packaging for medical supplies and food. Her plant did not shut down, and she ended up testing positive. Her experience was very asymptomatic and she was fortunate, especially while being pregnant. My grandpa was supposed to go on a European cruise, which was eventually canceled; thankfully, because he was supposed to go to Italy, one of the hardest hit countries.

I think the biggest impact was on my uncle's family. He is a restaurant manager. First, the restaurant shut down completely. Then, it opened for takeout only, but they experienced a pay cut and work schedule change. When the DHM allowed restaurants to fully open back up, he ended up catching the coronavirus. He went immediately into self-quarantine, and two days later, my aunt (his wife) and cousin (his daughter) both came down with symptoms. They monitored their symptoms closely--primarily body aches and fatigue--and were slowly able to recover without hospitalization.

Throughout this all, there's been a lot of change. We've all spent a lot of time in the house. We cook at home a lot more than normal. When we do go out of the house, we always wear a mask, respect social distancing, and wash our hands immediately. We've limited everything to the essentials. My parents' work changed. I had two aunts, an uncle, and a cousin all test positive. I haven't seen my great grandpa since March 13th. But at the end of the day, I will take all of this if it means my family is safe and sound. We've done our best to make the most of the time we've had together. We have our moments but to keep us all safe, we'll take those moments.

For Speaking Engagements, Book Signings,
Appearances, and Interviews...

Contact

NOAHS ARK PUBLISHING SERVICE
8549 Wilshire Blvd., Suite 1442
Beverly Hills, CA 90211

noahsarkpublishing@gmail.com
2020kidsunited@gmail.com

noahsarkpublishing.com

f www.facebook.com/laval.belle

 @lavalbelle

Made in the USA
Middletown, DE
25 October 2020